FROM THE BESTSELLING AUTHOR
OF WTF TO OMG, HAPPY ON PURPOSE AND THE
GRATITUDE TRANSFORMATION JOURNAL

ANNUAL LIFE REVIEW

WORKBOOK

JENNIFER SPARKS

LIFE STRATEGIST, AUTHOR, SPEAKER
WWW.JENNIFERSPARKS.CA

Attention Coaches and Group Facilitators

Should you wish to purchase Annual Life Review in multiple copies for group events, please email jennysparks@hotmail.ca directly for bulk order discounts.

Disclaimer

You undertake the activities in this book at your own risk.
If you end up happy, it is not my fault!

ISBN: 978-1-988675-73-2
STOKE Publishing

Contents

Introduction

This Annual Life Review can be done at any point in the year. For the sake of discussion in this workbook, we will assume that you are reflecting on your life sometime in November/December/January as you move into a new calendar year. The fundamental objective of this review process is to take the time to be reflective and open about what has worked well for you in the previous year and what has not so that you can better plan for the upcoming year. While I use this process in conjunction with the LIFEMAP Infinity Planning System, you can use your own planning system when scheduling your action items in your calendar.

How To Use This Annual Review

- Block off time in your calendar to do this review each year. If this is the first time you are doing this activity, look ahead a year and book time in your calendar to do it again next year. For example, I usually begin doing this process in November each year to start thinking about what I need to get done before the calendar year is over, and then I focus on getting those things wrapped up! I finish the process in late December as the new year rolls in and then start fresh in January with a clean slate and a clear vision forward. I am also in a heightened state of self-awareness.
- If you have a spouse or a partner, make sure you include them in this process. It can be a great way to build a connection and check-in with one another.
- If you have older children, don't leave them out! This is an opportunity to include them in the process and teach them how to use their own information to create more self-awareness, happiness, and a clear vision for their own lives.

There is space provided for you to answer the questions and make reflective notes so that this information can all be kept in one place. This makes it easier next year to review any previous considerations and notes.

What Do You Examine?

The annual review will examine many facets of your life. When you are reflecting, you will explore the following:

- **Career/Work (SAHM):** What you do to earn a living, contribute to the family, or fulfill a sense of purpose. In the case of a partnership, where one is home with kids, your unpaid work counts here too!
- **Finances**: Financial information, updated Wills, insurance, investments, retirement, budgets, and spending habits.
- **Physical Environment**: This is about anywhere you spend time—the car, office, home, and so forth.
- **Personal Growth:** This is about what you do to learn more about yourself. Personal growth can be learning, counseling, exploration, coaching, and so on.
- **Health and Wellness**: What do you do to take care of yourself? Self-care is more than massages and pedicures, as the doctor and dentist appointments matter too! Nutrition, movement, mental, emotional, and physical health all fall under here.
- **Romance or Community**: Are you connected in a network of support? Are you part of something beyond yourself?
- **Relationships**: Your key relationships – if you choose to place partner/romantic relationship in this umbrella, then you can use number six for community focus. If you want to keep the romance on its own, your community relationships can fit in here.
- **Spirituality**: Religion, philosophy, and anything that fills your energetic tank.

After working through these life areas, you will move into some additional reflective questions.

Materials

Please have the following items on hand.

- Access to your current calendar or planning system.
- Access to your next year's calendar or planning system. [If you are a client of mine, your LIFEMAP Infinity Planner should be at your beck and call. LIFEMAP Planners are available at www.thelifemapplanner.com. I advise the spiral-bound version.]
- Any calendars for extracurricular events, dates for events yet to book, and anything you have already committed to for the upcoming year.
- Sharp pencils and eraser. Pens.
- If you are one who likes stationery – sticky notes, highlighters, and so on.
- Time cleared in your day/week to focus on this review.
- Once you have moved through this process the first time, you will have a much better idea of what you want on hand for next time. You could make it easier for yourself by having a collection system (a simple folder works) for gathering papers throughout the year, so you have it come review time.
- Kindness to self. As you move through this process the first time, you will learn about the process and yourself. Save the judgment for another time. We can only master what we measure, and with this review, you are taking that first step. Your intentions are about to get crystal clear.

Let's get started!

Assessment

Without overthinking, please rate each area of your life from 0-10. If you score something a 0, you feel like this area is not going well. If you score that life area a 10, then you feel like it is going fantastic!

Work	Financial
0 – 1 – 2 – 3 – 4 – 5 – 6 – 7 – 8 – 9 – 10	0 – 1 – 2 – 3 – 4 – 5 – 6 – 7 – 8 – 9 – 10
Physical Environment	**Personal Growth**
0 – 1 – 2 – 3 – 4 – 5 – 6 – 7 – 8 – 9 – 10	0 – 1 – 2 – 3 – 4 – 5 – 6 – 7 – 8 – 9 – 10
Health and Wellness	**Community (or Romance)**
0 – 1 – 2 – 3 – 4 – 5 – 6 – 7 – 8 – 9 – 10	0 – 1 – 2 – 3 – 4 – 5 – 6 – 7 – 8 – 9 – 10
Relationships (Family and /or Romance)	**Spirituality**
0 – 1 – 2 – 3 – 4 – 5 – 6 – 7 – 8 – 9 – 10	0 – 1 – 2 – 3 – 4 – 5 – 6 – 7 – 8 – 9 – 10

*I would like to note here that if you do **not** have a partner at this time, but this is ideal for you at this time, then score accordingly. Being single doesn't mean you get an automatic 0 score. There may be times in your life where being single is the absolute best thing for you, and it makes you feel amazing! How you score your life areas is ABOUT HOW YOU FEEL about them, not what other people tell you how to feel about them.

Imagine

Imagine that a year has passed and you are sitting here doing your assessment again; what would you like to see for scores in the various areas of your life this time next year? Go ahead and score yourself AS IF you are 12 months in the future and you have made significant changes in your life to allow improvements in your scores.

In other words, **how do you want things to shift over the next year?**

Work	Financial
0 – 1– 2 – 3 – 4 – 5 – 6 – 7 – 8 – 9 – 10	0 – 1– 2 – 3 – 4 – 5 – 6 – 7 – 8 – 9 – 10
Physical Environment	**Personal Growth**
0 – 1– 2 – 3 – 4 – 5 – 6 – 7 – 8 – 9 – 10	0 – 1– 2 – 3 – 4 – 5 – 6 – 7 – 8 – 9 – 10
Health and Wellness	**Community (or Romance)**
0 – 1– 2 – 3 – 4 – 5 – 6 – 7 – 8 – 9 – 10	0 – 1– 2 – 3 – 4 – 5 – 6 – 7 – 8 – 9 – 10
Relationships (Family and /or Romance)	**Spirituality**
0 – 1– 2 – 3 – 4 – 5 – 6 – 7 – 8 – 9 – 10	0 – 1– 2 – 3 – 4 – 5 – 6 – 7 – 8 – 9 – 10

Please keep in mind that you are striving for your life to be approached from a holistic perspective. If you have success in the financial area and a great career but your relationships and health are in shambles, there is likely a problem (or there will be one eventually). You can't spend all that money from the grave, and broken relationships aren't going to bring you any joy! Make sure that you look at all life areas and think about what you would like to see in terms of change in each area.

What May Need To Change?

What might need to be changed in terms of how you spend your time, energy, and focus on approaching life from a more holistic perspective? Please think in terms of small daily changes that you could make that would change a given life area's trajectory. For example, walking daily for 30 minutes (to improve your health), automating a savings plan (to help your finances), or scheduling a monthly lunch date with your mother/child/best friend (to work on staying connected in your relationships.)

_____
_____
_____
_____
_____
_____
_____
_____
_____
_____
_____
_____
_____
_____
_____
_____
_____
_____
_____

How Can You Move The Needle?

Now, as you move through the rest of these activities, please keep in mind what things YOU need to change and what actions YOU will need to take to move the needle in these various life areas. If you are to see your scores improve, ACTION will be required on your part. ACTION may be consciously NOT taking action on an item and letting it go, and it may mean consciously TAKING ACTION where you normally would not.

- What will you need to let go of?
- What could you use more of in your life?
- What could you use less of in your life?
- What wisdom have you acquired this year that will allow you to avoid roadblocks in the upcoming year?
- Were you too busy doing things that didn't really matter because you were not focused? (Busy versus productive/sabotaging behaviors and mindsets, etc.)
- How could you invest that energy and focus differently?
- How do you want to feel next year that you didn't feel this year?
- What do you need to STOP doing?

LOOKING BACK

Please take some time to flip through your calendar, diary, or planning system for the last year and make a note of all of the major life events, people, and activities that took place over the last year. This would include trips you took, major life events (moves, illnesses, births, marriages, losses, career changes, etc.), family functions, and so forth.

Sort them into this chart as you flip week by week in last year's planner.

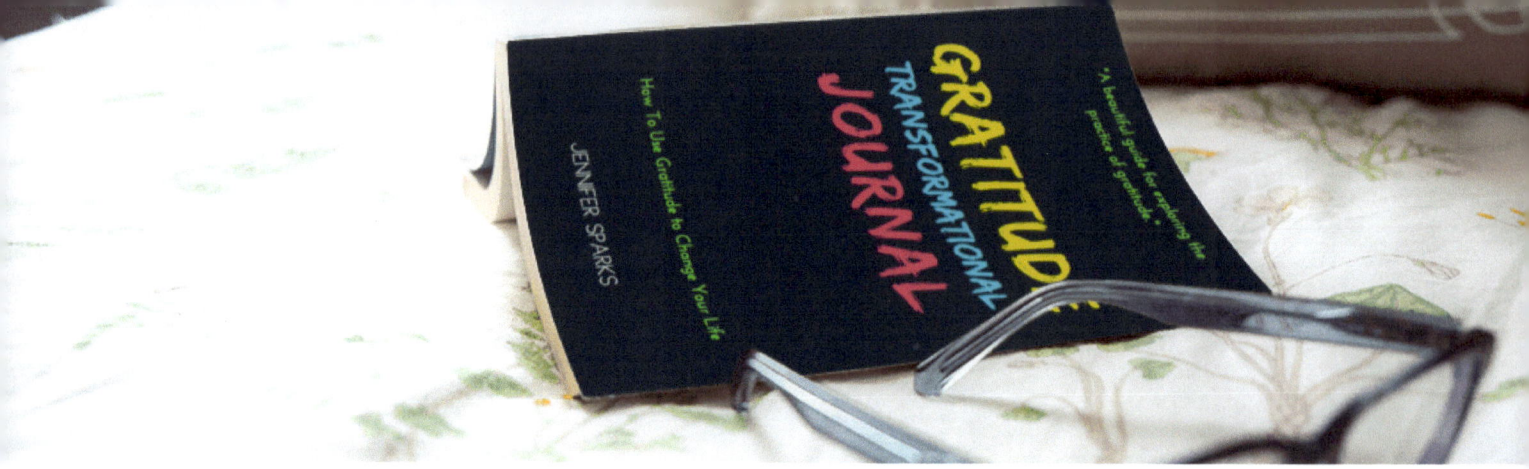

JOYFUL Events, People, Activities	CHALLENGING Events, People, Activities

JOYFUL Events, People, Activities	CHALLENGING Events, People, Activities

Reflect

WHAT ARE YOUR TOP FIVE JOYS AND CHALLENGES?

How do you feel about your list?

_____

_____

_____

_____

_____

What top 5 items in each list brought you the most JOY and the greatest CHALLENGES? (This is kind of a big picture look at events, people, and activities that bring you joy and stress.)

TOP FIVE JOYFUL Events, People, Activities	TOP FIVE CHALLENGING Events, People, Activities

Schedule The Joy

AND SHOW UP FOR YOURSELF

JOYFUL PLANNING

If any of these items can be repeated, grab your planner for the upcoming year and start scheduling these items in it (or move this note to the back Action Items pages of this workbook so you can schedule them later). For example, if Girl's Weekend is still a positive and joyful experience, then get the dates for next year and schedule it in! If spending a week at a rental cabin with your kids away from it all was joyful family time, book the cabin (or another adventure) and get it in your book! Budget out the expenses and payment plans if bookings are required. Look at loyalty points and spend out the balances. Put the pleasure in your life before the "other stuff" crowds out the time for you to do these things that bring you joy!

AVOIDING UNNECESSARY CHALLENGES

For the items that brought you too much stress, you will want to CONSCIOUSLY AVOID doing them again. Some of these may be touchy subjects and will require some conversations to clearly state your feelings and boundaries on your time, energy, and focus.

Is the family reunion too stressful or dysfunctional? Opt-out. Attend every second year. Visit family in other ways. You get to decide what you want to tolerate and what you do not. If it is your spouse's side of the family and they want to attend, it may be time to negotiate and come up with a compromise for each party.

- Be open to having hard but respectful conversations.
- Think about your personal boundaries and be prepared to communicate them.
- Be prepared to listen to other people's concerns, boundaries, and feelings.

Once you have scheduled your JOYFUL items, you need to SHOW UP FOR YOURSELF and do your best not to cancel them because your plans change. This is a sacred space in your planner.

At the end of the year, if you fail to show up for yourself and you DO NOT do these JOYFUL things, how will you feel? Protect your JOY!

What Worked? What Did Not?

(This is a more detailed look at events, people, daily habits, and activities that bring you joy and stress daily.)

At this point, look at **what worked well and what did not work well** in the various life areas on a more detailed level (like the daily habits and rituals you have) and schedule MORE OF WHAT WORKS into your days, weeks, and months ahead.

- If you realize that starting your day at 6 am with a workout served you in fabulous ways, then looking ahead at the year, you will want that to continue that daily habit/ritual. Schedule that to be part of your days. Go ahead, grab your planner (or indicate to do so in the Action Items).

- If you can see that you didn't do anything that helped you learn about yourself or move your personal growth forward, you can make sure to schedule in time to research some things you would like to do this year, and then you can take action and schedule them in your planner.

- If you realize that not checking on your finances regularly caused you to disconnect from what you were spending and earning, then you may wish to have a weekly money date with your online credit card statements and bank balances to stay on top of your debt reduction/savings/retirement plan. The only way to make sure this will actually happen (and not just be wishful thinking) is to schedule the money dates in your planner!

- If you realized that binge-watching Netflix series until the wee hours of the morning sabotaged your ability to wake as planned, had you hitting the snooze and then running around like crazy to avoid being late for work, you would need to come up with an alternative plan. Besides, setting an emotional tone for the day that will be hard to escape, you are sabotaging your ability to stay focused on your plan!

What Worked? What Did Not?

Considering what you realize works well for you, **grab your planner and schedule what you want to make a part of each day, week, or month.**

If you are using the LIFEMAP Planner, for example, many tools are already embedded. On Sundays, you have a Day of Alignment to review the previous week and look ahead and plan the next one; you have places for daily habit stacking, you have a place to note daily intention. If you do not have the LIFEMAP Planner, sticky notes can work well for scheduling items that you can move forward once you have done them on a given day, week, or month. Or, go ahead and write them into your planner.

It may seem like overkill and repetitive to plan out each day but don't take for granted that you will always REMEMBER that your intention was to workout each morning or to have weekly lunch dates with your spouse/partner because life gets busy. If you do not PROTECT your routines and plans, they dissolve into chaos.

Also, consider scheduling in BUFFER time. The odd day/weekend where you keep it clear to catch up on the spillover from curve balls that ultimately come our way. It is absolutely okay to schedule downtime too. Maybe you keep all Sundays as "no work" zones! Or every third weekend is kept open for a spontaneous adventure!

This is your life - take complete ownership!

Examine Daily Habits + Routines

LIFE AREA REFLECTIONS: WORK/CAREER

What <u>worked well</u> for you this year in your work/career habits?

_____
_____
_____
_____
_____

What <u>did not work well</u> for you this year in your work/career habits?

_____
_____
_____
_____
_____

LIFE AREA REFLECTIONS: FINANCES

What <u>worked well</u> for you this year in your financial habits?

_____
_____
_____
_____
_____

What <u>did not work well</u> for you this year in your financial habits?

_____
_____
_____
_____
_____

Examine Daily Habits + Routines

LIFE AREA REFLECTIONS: PHYSICAL ENVIRONMENT

What worked well for you this year in your environmental habits?

_____
_____
_____
_____
_____

What did not work well for you this year in your environmental habits?

_____
_____
_____
_____
_____

LIFE AREA REFLECTIONS: PERSONAL GROWTH

What worked well for you this year in your personal growth habits?

_____
_____
_____
_____

What did not work well for you this year in your personal growth habits?

_____
_____
_____
_____

Examine Daily Habits + Routines

LIFE AREA REFLECTIONS: HEALTH AND WELLNESS

What worked well for you this year in your health and wellness habits?

_____
_____
_____
_____
_____

What did not work well for you this year in your health and wellness habits?

_____
_____
_____
_____
_____

LIFE AREA REFLECTIONS: ROMANCE AND COMMUNITY

What worked well for you this year in your romance and community habits?

_____
_____
_____
_____

What did not work well for you this year in your romance and community habits?

_____
_____
_____
_____
_____

Examine Daily Habits + Routines

LIFE AREA REFLECTIONS: RELATIONSHIPS

What worked well for you this year in your relationship habits?
_____
_____
_____
_____
_____

What did not work well for you this year in your relationship habits?
_____
_____
_____
_____
_____

LIFE AREA REFLECTIONS: SPIRITUALITY

What worked well for you this year in your spiritual habits?
_____
_____
_____
_____
_____

What did not work well for you this year in your spiritual habits?
_____
_____
_____
_____
_____

Choosing To Struggle

It's true. Sometimes, we unconsciously CHOOSE to struggle when we do not have to. We seem unable to just "let it be easy."

Was your year more of a struggle than it was joyful, or was it the other way around? Explain/Reflect.

_____
_____
_____
_____
_____
_____
_____
_____

Also, please consider this...

In the areas where your life was a struggle, did you ignore or follow your intuition? In the areas where your life was more joyful, did you ignore or follow your intuition?

_____
_____
_____
_____
_____
_____
_____
_____

Letting Go

Look at each part of your life and brainstorm a list of things you want to **leave behind in each life section** as you move forward into a new year. Anything that caused you grief, didn't serve you, increased your stress more than it brought value to your life, and so forth. If you are into the woo, write all this stuff down again so you can burn it safely. It is helpful to leave a copy in this book for next year's reference. You may discover next year that a pattern has been long-standing and you need some extra help to break it.

What I Am Leaving Behind

Career/Work	Financial
Physical Environment	**Personal Growth**
Health and Wellness	**Community (or Romance)**
Relationships (Family and /or Romance)	**Spirituality**

What Did You Learn?

Using the list you created in the WHAT I AM LEAVING BEHIND activity, look at your items, and try to extract any nuggets of wisdom you have gainned because of these experiences.

- Have you learned valuable lessons from these experiences that you want to carry forward?
- Are there things you are grateful for despite the painful experience you had to go through?

The idea here is, let go of (or burn) what is no longer serving you but to take the learnings and wisdom with you so next year has you better prepared!

If you don't learn the lesson, you get to repeat the struggle!

It will likely be a less successful year for you if you simply hope and wish for a better year. PLAN A BETTER YEAR!

Take a moment to think about what you learned from the good, the bad, and the ugly.

These lessons will come in handy as you move forward and help you from repeating things you would like to avoid.

What Did You Learn?

Career/Work	Financial
Physical Environment	**Personal Growth**
Health and Wellness	**Community (or Romance)**
Relationships (Family and /or Romance)	**Spirituality**

Looking Ahead

Take a look into the future and think about how you want to feel in the various areas of your life. If you have done my VISION QUEST Workbook, this is the same type of activity, but your focus is on what you are bringing forward into your life. Think about all areas of your life and brainstorm how you want to feel in each area.

HOW DO YOU WANT TO FEEL IN EACH AREA OF YOUR LIFE?

Often, we focus on goals, but goals are simply how we try to achieve a feeling.

For example, I may have the goal of running a marathon (completing the 42.2k), but there is also a feeling I am hoping the experience brings me as well. Perhaps I want to feel fit and strong or dedicated and accomplished. If I spend the day in and day out working towards a goal that I think will make me feel a certain way, but when I achieve the goal, the feeling is nowhere to be found, I would have missed out on enjoying the journey, and my target goal didn't actually bring me what I desired.

Thinking about how you want to feel will help you understand more about yourself and your desires. When picking goals for next year, you will also want to think about how much joy there will be in the journey and if it will help you feel the way you want to feel.

How Do You Want To Feel?

Career/Work	Financial
Physical Environment	**Personal Growth**
Health and Wellness	**Community (or Romance)**
Relationships (Family and /or Romance)	**Spirituality**

New Life Experiences

Looking at the life areas again, brainstorm what new things or experiences you would like to have in each area? Stretch! Put down things that make you giddy, excited, and a little uncomfortable! Then, schedule in some actions you can take to start making them real.

Career/Work	Financial
Physical Environment	**Personal Growth**
Health and Wellness	**Community (or Romance)**
Relationships (Family and /or Romance)	**Spirituality**

Reflection Questions

Where are you going this year and who is coming with you?

_____
_____
_____
_____
_____

When you are living a passionate and purpose-filled life, it looks like ...

_____
_____
_____
_____
_____

When you are living a passionate and purposed fill life, you feel ...

_____
_____
_____
_____
_____

What do you need to believe about your life, self, the world, etc., for your dreams to come true?

_____
_____
_____
_____
_____
_____

Reflection Questions

What is the cost of you not going after your dreams? What is the actual cost of staying put? (more stress, less satisfaction, lack of joy and excitement...)

_____

_____

_____

_____

_____

_____

_____

_____

_____

_____

_____

_____

_____

_____

_____

_____

_____

_____

_____

_____

_____

_____

Reflection Questions

Think about how different your life would be if you took immediate and decisive action on your dreams.

Write down things you would gain(ie, freedom, joy, inspiration, confidence).

_____
_____
_____
_____
_____

Now, think about not taking any action, and what will your life be like in a year? What is the cost of not taking action? What do you lose out on? What will you need to tolerate if you don't change things?

_____
_____
_____
_____
_____
_____
_____
_____
_____
_____
_____
_____
_____
_____
_____

Reflection Questions

What are the top five things you want to change for the upcoming year?

_____
_____
_____
_____
_____
_____
_____
_____
_____
_____

What are the first steps in making sure you take action on these desired changes?

_____
_____
_____
_____
_____
_____
_____
_____
_____
_____
_____
_____
_____
_____
_____

Reflection Questions

You may have an inner voice that is trying to nudge you in a different direction, what is it saying, and why are you not convinced it is safe to go that way?

_____
_____
_____
_____
_____

If you were not afraid you would ... (change careers, quit a job, leave a relationship, ask someone out, sell all your belongings ...)

_____
_____
_____
_____
_____

What does your ideal day look like? How do you spend your time, energy, focus and money? Who is with you? Where do you live? What is your daily schedule like?

_____
_____
_____
_____
_____
_____
_____
_____
_____

Reflection Questions

What does your ideal year look like? Where would you live, travel, or visit? When would you take holidays, and what would you do with them? Would you live in a house, condo, or go van life? How would you spend your time, energy, money, and focus? Who would be with you or in your life?

_____
_____
_____
_____
_____
_____
_____
_____
_____
_____
_____
_____
_____
_____
_____
_____
_____
_____
_____
_____
_____
_____
_____

Reflection Questions

Does feeling uncertain about an outcome or an action keep you from taking the next step? What if you took the next step anyway?

_____

_____

_____

_____

_____

How can you take that next step now?

_____

_____

_____

_____

_____

What things need to happen in the next year for you to feel positive and pleased with your progress?

_____

_____

_____

_____

_____

_____

_____

_____

_____

_____

_____

Reflection Questions

What are your BIGGEST excuses for staying stuck? (Do you blame others? Do you consider yourself a victim in certain situations? Are you afraid?) Explain.

_____
_____
_____
_____
_____
_____
_____
_____
_____

How do you usually keep yourself from taking action?

_____
_____
_____
_____
_____
_____
_____
_____
_____
_____
_____
_____
_____
_____

Take Action

You have reflected on the past year, and you have come up with some things that you can do to help you plan a great year!

But, if you do not take action on these great ideas, this time next year, you will be kicking yourself for letting autopilot take over.

- You deserve to create a life you love.
- You know what needs to change.
- You know what works and what doesn't.
- You know how you want to feel.
- You know what new habits you need to create and what ones do not serve you.
- You know what brings you joy and what causes struggle and stress.
- You have identified some new life experiences you want to enjoy!
- You can schedule some new actions into your planner and show up for yourself.
- You can do the things in your planner, even when you don't feel like it.

This is where the rubber meets the road. YOU MUST SHOW UP FOR YOURSELF.

In the pages that follow, you wrote down ACTION ITEMS to take towards this life you imagine for yourself. Now, TAKE ACTION.

Get your planner out, grab your phone, make the calls, book the tickets, call the people, get the dates, SCHEDULE these beautiful things into your life, and make magic happen!

All the best to you for your new year!

Jennifer Sparks

Action Items to Schedule

Use this space to make a list of things you want to schedule into your upcoming year.

_____
_____
_____
_____
_____
_____
_____
_____
_____
_____
_____
_____
_____
_____
_____
_____
_____
_____
_____
_____
_____
_____
_____
_____
_____

Action Items to Schedule

_____
_____
_____
_____
_____
_____
_____
_____
_____
_____
_____
_____
_____
_____
_____
_____
_____
_____
_____
_____
_____
_____
_____
_____
_____
_____
_____
_____
_____

Action Items to Schedule

_____
_____
_____
_____
_____
_____
_____
_____
_____
_____
_____
_____
_____
_____
_____
_____
_____
_____
_____
_____
_____
_____
_____
_____
_____
_____
_____
_____

Action Items to Schedule

About Jennifer

Jennifer is a life strategist, author, and speaker. She has been a personal development junkie for over 15 years. She has two grown children and is excited to be entering into a new phase of life.

Jennifer has several group coaching programs and enjoys helping her clients work through fears, blocks, and limiting belief systems.

To learn more about Jennifer, please visit www.jennifersparks.ca.

Jennifer's books can be found on Amazon. You can follow her on IG @jennifersparks.inspirethefire

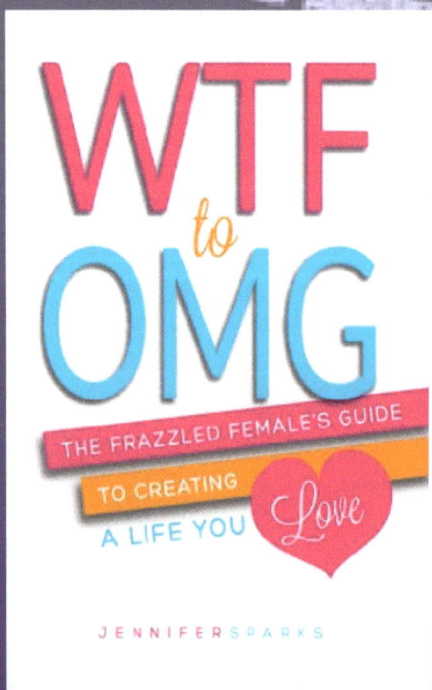

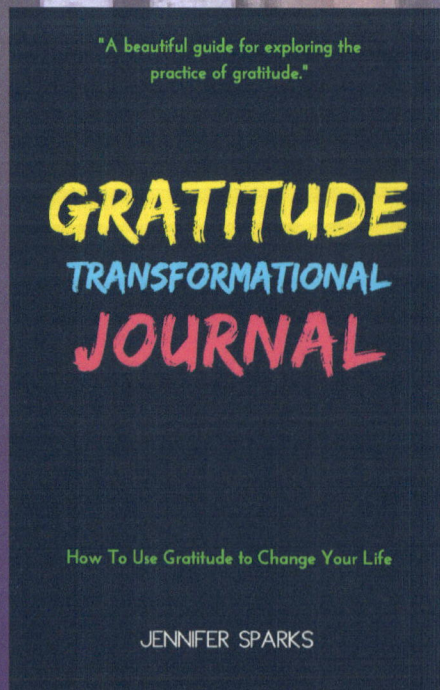

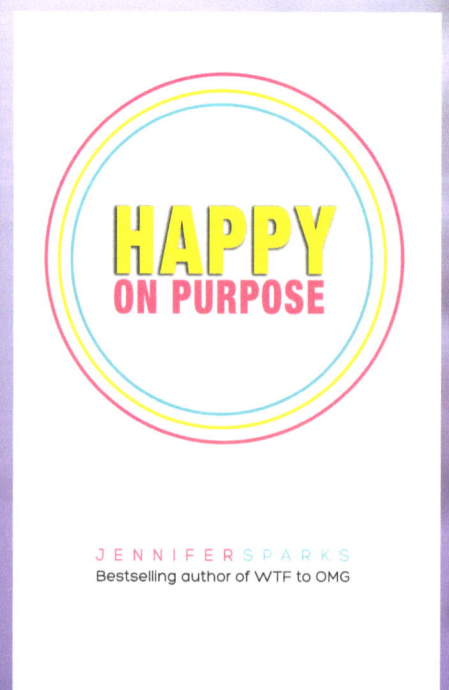

WTF to OMG
THE FRAZZLED FEMALE'S GUIDE TO CREATING A LIFE YOU Love

JENNIFER SPARKS

GRATITUDE TRANSFORMATIONAL JOURNAL

"A beautiful guide for exploring the practice of gratitude."

How To Use Gratitude to Change Your Life

JENNIFER SPARKS

HAPPY ON PURPOSE

JENNIFER SPARKS
Bestselling author of WTF to OMG